Contents

Introduction

'LONDON IS A CITY OF SECRET PLACES', said the architect, painter and author Sir Hugh Casson. If you have never seen the place in this light, this book will provide the evidence, describing an underground London that few people know and even fewer ever see. In it you will read about the capital's lost rivers, wells and spas, also the extensive man-made tunnel systems that serve London's communications, power and water undertakings, which support the everyday operation of the capital.

In these pages you will also discover the hidden world of bunkers, control centres, civilian shelters and even factories that were constructed under conditions of great secrecy to maintain 'due functioning' of the nation's government under conditions of emergency or war.

Some of the subjects of this book were once highly confidential, particularly those constructed during the Second World War and the Cold War era. Thanks to the 'peace dividend' period of the 1990s many of these former secrets were 'declassified' and opened up to researchers who knew where to look. By no means everything was revealed, however, and any anarchists or terrorists will not discover any current secrets in these pages. This book has been written with due regard to, and in full compliance with, the provisions of the Official Secrets Act. All sources quoted are in the public domain and no use has been made of currently classified material.

A number of the locations described in these pages are open to visitors and these are listed at the end of each chapter. For security, health and safety or other reasons it is not possible to visit the other places. Finally, two points to note: a book of this size cannot cover all of London's rich variety of subterranea and this is purely a personal selection of some of the most fascinating and unusual locations. Also, a few of the most interesting illustrations are taken from old documents and are not up to today's reproduction standards.

A ghost train on the Post Office Railway? You certainly won't see any trains running on its mothballed tracks today but there was an intensive service when this trick photo was taken in 1974.

Highgate
Caen Wood
Ponds
Parliament Hill
Straws Cas.
Hampstead
SEVEN SISTERS ROAD
HOLLOWAY ROAD
LEA BRIDGE
Kentish Town
ST. PAUL'S RD
Dalston
New R.
ROAD
KINGSLAND ROAD
ADELAIDE RD
Primrose Hill
CAMDEN
YORK RD
UPPER ST.
Barrow Hill
Camden Town
St. John's Wood
REGENTS PARK
Holebourne
Kings Cross
MAIDA VALE
PARK RD
GOSWELL RD
Clerkenwell
Westbourne
Marylebone
EUSTON RD
Holborn
St. Paul's
CITY WALL
Wall Brook
WHITECHAPEL
BAKER STR.
GLOUC. ROAD
FLEET ST.
COMMER
dington
OXFORD STR.
Tower
Tyebourne
R. Tha
HYDE PARK
PICCADILLY
Blackfriars Br.
BAYSWATER
THE MALL
Serpentine
Westminster Br.
KENSINGTON RD
KNIGHTSBRIDGE
Abbey
SLOANE ST.
I. of Thorney
OLD KENT ROAD
WALWORTH RD
Bridge Cr.
Lambeth
FULHAM ROAD
KING'S RD
Pimlico
Vauxhall Br.
R. Neckinger
Chelsea Br.
Peckha
Denmark Hill
ulham
QUEEN
WANDSWORTH RD
CLAPHAM ROAD
BRIXTON ROAD
Battersea
Clapham
Herne Hill
LORDSHIP LANE
YORK RD
ACRE LA.
Falcon Br.
Brixton
TULSEHILL
R. Effra
Wandsworth
R. Wandle
GARRATT LANE
TRINITY ROAD
Balham
PALACE RD
Dulwich
Tooting
Streatham
Sydenha

Unseen rivers and hidden wells

ASK MOST PEOPLE how many rivers flow through London – they would answer only one, the Thames. In fact there are several more: the Fleet River, the Tyburn, the Effra Brook and other 'lost' rivers. These waters are still flowing, but nowadays they are enclosed in pipes underground. However, during 2008 the Mayor of London announced that he was planning to bring sixteen of London's lost waterways to the surface in an ambitious vision that would start in the suburbs but include 'ornamental stretches' of inner London rivers if possible.

These long-forgotten watercourses do not appear on normal maps and street plans, except where their identity survives in the name of streets (Fleet Street for instance) and of districts such as Holborn (the hollow waterway) and Marylebone (church of St Mary next to the bourne). Tracing the exact path of these streams would be very difficult were it not for the careful researches of historians. Fortunately a number of books and websites now make it easy for anyone wishing to study these former flows (recommended further reading may be found at our website – see page 79)

OPPOSITE: A map of London's underground streams and rivers, all of which are natural except the New River. The watercourse shown as the Holebourne is more commonly known as the Fleet River.

The Fleet, also known as the Holebourn and the River of Wells, is probably the best known of these. It rises from the most southerly of Highgate Ponds and runs, via King's Cross and Farringdon Street (which more or less follows the line of the old valley of the stream), to the River Thames by Blackfriars Bridge. After being treated as a rubbish dump, the section near the Thames became a stinking cesspit and was covered over in 1760. By the end of the eighteenth century its northern section had ceased to be an open stream running through the country, and in 1855 became a sewer. At one time the central section was also known as the 'river of wells' on account of the numerous healing (and other) wells adjacent to its banks. These include St Chad's Well, Bagnigge Wells, Black Mary's Hole, Pancras Wells, Clerkenwell (originally Clerks Well) and several more.

Bridewell Dock stood at the south end of the Fleet River, where it emptied itself into the Thames (where New Bridge Street runs today). At the time this view was drawn in 1666 coal-barges could come up the Fleet as far as Holborn Bridge, where Holborn Viaduct stands today.

Although now contained in a sewer, the Fleet still managed to burst its way out in 1862 during the construction of the Metropolitan Line of the London underground. Between Farringdon Road (seen here) and King's Cross the new railway line was flooded to a depth of 10 feet.

Rivers south of the Thames that now run underground include the Effra, the Falcon Brook, and the strange-sounding Neckinger. A more westerly stream was the Westbourne, which flows from Hampstead through Kilburn, near Paddington station, through Hyde Park and Knightsbridge to enter the

Today the Fleet is encased in iron pipes, as seen in this view from the 1860s at the time the Midland Railway's station at St Pancras was being constructed.

OPPOSITE TOP: Roman art and gas lighting were the order of the day at London's Roman Bath in 1900 when this somewhat retouched photograph was taken. On this occasion the photographer managed to capture some additional classical beauty in his picture.

Thames at Chelsea. It is probably the most visible of London's underground rivers, simply because it crosses the Circle Line of the Underground at Sloane Square station, where you can see it – encased in a rectangular iron tube – from the platforms. The Tyburn or Tyebourne Brook rises in South Hampstead and ran along Marylebone Lane and west of Bond Street (where a feature in the basement of Grays Mews is said to be a replica of this lost river). Near the present St James's Park the brook divided into three branches, reaching the Thames in Westminster.

The most notable lost river in the City of London is the Walbrook or Wallbrook, which was already built over in 1598. Rising in Moorfields, it flowed past the site of today's Bank of England and Mansion House to the Thames at Dowgate Hill, off Upper Thames Street. It is said that boats used once to ascend this little creek as far as Bucklersbury and when Queen Victoria Street was constructed in 1862 an old craft was found preserved in the mud.

PLACES TO VISIT

Grays Mews antiques market

Location: 58 Davies Street and 1–7 Davies Mews, W1K 5AB.

Still exists? Yes.

Accessible? Yes.

A re-creation of the Tyburn Brook flows through the basement of these premises (ask the staff if you need directions).

Roman Bath

Location: 5 Strand Lane, WC2R 2NA (reached via an alley on Surrey Street).

Still exists? Yes.

RIGHT: This publicity leaflet of the 1930s asserts an earlier construction date than many of today's experts are prepared to accept.

BELOW: Back in the 1970s the admission price was 5 pence. Now it's an even bigger bargain as it doesn't cost a penny!

"LINKS WITH THE PAST."

The Old Roman Spring Bath

Nearly 2,000 years old.

Yesterday.

At Sloane Square underground station the 'lost' river Westbourne flows encased in this iron conduit above the platforms.

Accessible? Yes, but by advance appointment only by calling 020 7641 5264. The bath is visible from the pathway through its window during daylight hours. According to its owners, the National Trust, the cold bath is believed to have Roman origins and was restored in the seventeenth century. Other opinion states it is almost certainly not Roman, especially as there is no other evidence of Roman habitation in the neighbourhood. It may have been part of Arundel House, a major residence that stood on the Strand.

The Westbourne at Sloane Square station, *c*. 1910.

In Victorian times cold plunges taken here were believed to improve health and Charles Dickens' character David Copperfield was a regular visitor.

Sloane Square underground station

Location: Sloane Square, SW1W 8BB.

Still exists? Yes.

Accessible? Yes.

The River Westbourne can be seen here encased in an iron conduit above the eastern end of the platforms. Although the station was bombed in 1940, no damage was sustained by the sewer.

Sewers, aquifers and hydraulics

SEWER SAGA

It would be easy to argue that sewers are the most important part of London's underground infrastructure. Although ancient Rome's *Cloaca Maxima* sewer system was first built around 600 BC London had to wait until the mid-1600s for its first sewer. What we might call serious sewer construction in London was the result of a number of public health scandals in the nineteenth century and was masterminded by the civil engineer Joseph Bazalgette (1819–91). Bazalgette has been credited with saving more lives than any other single Victorian public official and the network of sewers that he designed was copied by many other cities throughout the world. As the book *The Great Stink of London* explains, two million people poured their sewage directly into the river until the Thames became 'absolutely pestilential'. Indeed, in the hot summer of 1858 the stink was so unbearable that members of Parliament and ministers were forced to leave the Houses of Parliament. Newspapers named the crisis 'The Great Stink', the public

OPPOSITE: Pipe subways such as this one running below Rosebery Avenue are more 'amenable' – if less spectacular – than the open brick channels of Victorian times. This one is accessed from under the bridge in Warner Street.

demanded action and within sixteen days MPs passed a law for constructing the additional sewers that Bazalgette had proposed.

Once the sewer system had been completed it was soon taken for granted by the public, who of course had no opportunity to see the actual sewer conduits, chambers and other paraphernalia of this malodorous underworld. Over the years, however, London's sewers have been celebrated in a number of magazine articles, which have turned up many interesting facts. Some sewers flow in vaulted channels 12 feet high, as an open stream, so to speak. Others are contained in pipes that run along the shared service subways that run beneath many central London streets and thoroughfares.

Far more spectacular is this waterfall under Ludgate Circus where a sewer cascaded into the old Fleet River. The somewhat retouched photo was taken in 1900.

Many coins are discovered on the clean stone floor of the piped subways; some were lost by accident, but others were dropped deliberately through the gratings by crooks who found it necessary to get rid of their 'evidence' rapidly. Many purses and wallets are found too, abandoned by the light fingered fraternity after extracting the valuable contents. Rats used to abound in London's sewers: 'At every few yards they dash past us, great fat fellows, twice as large as the ordinary outdoor rat', gushed one journalist. Another writer attested to the boldness (and stupidity) of these rodents, stating that one had been known to snatch a lighted candle held in front of a drain from a man's hand.

Many sewer tunnels were signposted just like the streets above ground. In this chamber below the junction of Holborn Circus and Charterhouse Street, works a cheerful lad in about 1900.

An interesting aside is that London's sewers continue to follow their traditional routes, regardless of alterations affecting the streets above. In 1900 *Harmsworth's Magazine* noted that a few historic spots that have long since disappeared above ground are still to be found below the pavement. For example, it would be a difficult task to find Poppins Court, redolent of Johnsonian memories, but it still exists in underground London.

So far we have discussed only the 'local' or street sewers of London, but these were only part of Bazalgette's plan. During his sixteen-year construction project he built not only 1,100 miles of street sewers, but also 82 miles of main intercepting sewers that collected the contents of the existing sewers and delivered them by gravity to pumping stations at Abbey Mills (on the north bank) and

Deptford (on the south). Giant pumping engines at these locations raised the sewage to the higher level of the outfall sewers, enabling gravity to carry the detritus to treatment works at Beckton and Crossness, where the sewage was stored in vast reservoirs and then released into the Thames at high tide. The entire network is still operated by Thames Water, extended as London has expanded. Although the huge steam pumps installed by Bazalgette have been replaced by modern electrically powered equipment, the original equipment at Crossness is being restored by the Crossness Engines Trust.

LONDON'S WATER SUPPLY

London's drinking water travels underground today and in fact has done so since 1613, when the New River was opened. This was a man-made channel constructed to carry spring water from Ware in Hertfordshire to London. Although the distance is only 20 miles, taking a path as the crow flies would involve requiring water to flow uphill, so the actual distance along the all-level route is twice as far. The

As late as 1800 the Fleet River was an open watercourse from its source as far as Holborn. This is King's Cross, where (leaking) wooden pipes for domestic drinking water cross the Fleet on a bridge.

London 'terminal' of this partly-underground channel is at New River Head in Clerkenwell. From here the water was distributed first by wooden pipes (made by removing the inner core of elm tree trunks) and subsequently in cast iron pipes. A central reservoir with sluice controls was built at the New River Head, with a subsidiary covered reservoir (built in 1709) in Claremont Square, near the Angel.

The New River, dug by more than two hundred labourers, was without doubt a momentous engineering feat of its day. Equally significant among created watercourses, but far less well known, is the London Ring Main water tunnel officially opened in 1994 by HM the Queen and completed two years ahead of schedule. It is the longest tunnel ever built in this country and also the largest capital project that Thames Water has ever undertaken. Yet hardly anyone has heard of it, despite some remarkable statistics and features. At 50 miles long, the tunnel

The New River at Harringay, north London. An entirely artificial watercourse, it opened in 1613, in the reign of James I, to bring fresh water to London from the River Lee at Ware and from springs at Great Amwell, Hertfordshire.

runs beneath the capital like an underground M25 motorway at an average depth of 130 feet, deeper than most lines on the London Underground. 'Motorway' is not altogether an illogical description, as the tunnel is wide enough for a car to pass through. Being built in a ring, water can flow in either direction and if a section is taken out of service for maintenance, supplies can still be delivered to every area of London. It does not provide new sources of water but improves the speed and efficiency of transferring supplies of drinking water across the capital. Water is moved by gravity, resulting in large energy savings as expensive overland pumping is reduced.

NEW TUNNELS

At the time of writing two new tunnels, each around 3 miles long, are being constructed to extend the Ring Main, for completion in 2010. One links Coppermills water treatment works to the Ring Main, connecting with existing mains at Stoke Newington and Thames Water's site at New River Head. The second tunnel feeds water from the Ring Main to an existing underground reservoir in Peckham at Honor Oak.

Another scheme, equally ambitious, is the Tideway Tunnel, which was given the go-ahead in March 2007. Its role is to mitigate a key problem facing sewer engineers, that of overflows. Street sewers carry both sewage and rainwater, which is why they are also called 'combined sewers'. Heavy rain storms can create significant overloads for the system and the Tideway Tunnel will capture millions of tonnes of storm sewage entering the tidal stretch of the River Thames, resulting in major improvements to river water quality. The project will involve the construction of London's deepest ever tunnels, running as deep as 250 feet beneath ground level for 20 miles beneath the River Thames, from Hammersmith in west London to Beckton in east London. An additional tunnel, the Lee Tunnel, will run for 4 miles from Abbey Mills in Stratford to Beckton. Both tunnels need to be deep enough to avoid London's existing underground infrastructure, such as tube train tunnels, existing sewers and cable tunnels. The tunnel will have enough capacity to store millions of litres of diluted sewage and transfer it to the Beckton Sewage Works for treatment. As well as having significant environmental benefits for the River Thames, the tunnel will provide London with a sewerage system fit for the twenty-first century and beyond.

WATER UNDER PRESSURE

Water has a remarkable property in that it is virtually incompressible, making it an ideal agent for transmitting power from one place to another. Today we use electricity for this purpose, but before this became widely available, hydraulic power – using water under high pressure transmitted in large pipes known as hydraulic mains – was king. Ironically, although these mains ran below ground (justifying their connection with subterranean London), the only visible evidence today for their existence is the remaining buildings above ground that supported what was for more than a century a vast power distribution network to thousands of hotels, shops, offices, mansion blocks, hotels, docks and factories. Hydraulic power played an important part in the operations of lifts and cranes, but there were many other processes that used pressurised water, such as

To many observers hydraulic mains looked no different from any other kind of large pipe. On this murky day around 1930 we see original cast-iron pipes with oval flange spigot-and-faucet joints being removed and replaced with new steel pipes using Victaulic joints. The location is Piccadilly, where now as then the number 38 bus takes you to Victoria.

baling cloth and paper in warehouses and for compressing scrap metal.

Water power in London was supplied by the London Hydraulic Power Company, which opened for business in 1871. Until the company closed in 1977, the company supplied water at a pressure of 700 pounds per square inch, day and night, all the year round, through some 150 (180 before the Second World War) miles of cast iron and steel hydraulic mains laid under the streets of London.

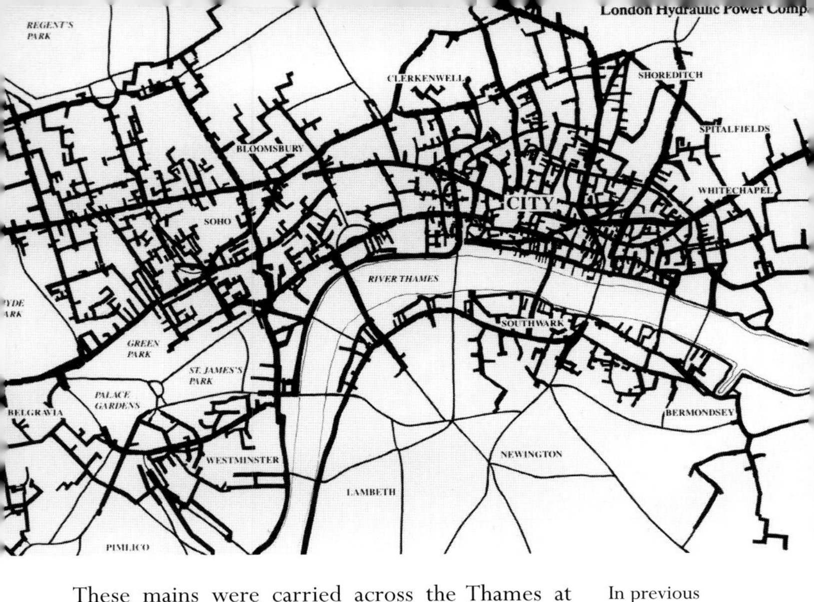

These mains were carried across the Thames at Vauxhall Bridge, Waterloo Bridge and Southwark Bridge, also crossing under the river through Rotherhithe Tunnel and the Tower Subway beneath the Pool of London. At its peak the company was pumping more than 1.6 billion gallons of water annually from five pumping stations. Hydraulic power raised the curtain at the Royal Opera House, rotated the turntable at the Coliseum, raised lifts at the Bank of England (and thousands of other offices and flats) and opened dock gates on the Thames. Another Shire publication, *Hydraulic Machines*, now out of print but readily available second-hand, describes these applications in more detail.

In previous times the high-pressure mains of the London Hydraulic Power Company served a vast number of streets in London's commercial districts. Today some of them still serve a purpose, carrying telecommunications cables.

For many years, up to the general adoption of small electric motors, hydraulic power was the simplest and most reliable means of operating a wide range of plant and machinery. However, wartime bomb damage, and the departure of many manufacturing firms from central London, led to a decline that ended when pumping ceased in 1977. Its network of pipes did not lie idle for long. Control of the company was acquired in 1981 by investors who recognised the importance of the pipe network for the coming generation of communications systems. The network of 150 miles of pipes, ducts and conduits was sold in 1985 to Mercury Communications Ltd, now owned by Cable & Wireless Ltd, and since that time many miles of optical fibre cable have been laid in this network.

The London Hydraulic Power Company never had a monopoly of hydraulic power generation and many dock and railway undertakings in London generated their own hydraulic power, using steam pumping engines and conspicuous 'accumulator' towers containing elevated tanks for storing this energy. A few such towers can still be seen, such as one close to the north end of Tower Bridge. Tower Bridge itself was operated by hydraulic power and the huge steam engines can still be seen in its engine room, now a museum. Once the London Hydraulic Power Company's mains spread out and provided reliable service most users abandoned their own compressors. Since the demise of the LHP Company the wheel has turned full circle, forcing users to install their own hydraulic plant or convert their hydraulically powered apparatus to electric motors.

OPPOSITE AND BELOW: Prospective customers were offered detailed street plans that showed every street served by hydraulic mains together with the location of all five pumping stations.

LONDON HYDRAULIC POWER COMPANY

(Incorporated by Acts of Parliament)

Offices

RENFORTH STREET, ROTHERHITHE, S.E.16.

Telephone: 01-237 0593/4/5

Telegrams

HYDRISTIC, SEDIST, LONDON

Telephone

~~WATERLOO 4541 (3 Lines)~~

If you are wondering what's left to see, the answer is not a great deal. A number of formerly hydraulic lifts were converted to electrical operation and a few of these must survive unrecognised. Valve box covers marked LHP adorn the pavements of some London streets and these record where the mains could be isolated by stop valves in a cast-iron box below. However, by far the most visible remains of hydraulic power are a number of accumulator towers that once acted as the water equivalent of a rechargeable electric battery. In addition, the Grade II*-listed Wapping Hydraulic Power Station on Wapping Wall has been transformed into a successful cultural amenity that has attracted international interest and has been compared favourably with the Tate Modern.

PLACES TO VISIT

Camden Town hydraulic accumulator tower

Location: East side of Gloucester Avenue, NW1 (north side of Regents Canal, just west of the railway line).
Still exists? Yes.
Accessible? No.

Claremont Square covered reservoir

Location: Claremont Square, N1 9LS.
Still exists? Yes.
Accessible? No, but the reservoir is visible from the street.
This covered reservoir is part of the New River system and is best viewed from the upper deck of a westbound bus from The Angel to King's Cross.

Clissold Park watercourse

Location: Green Lanes, N4 2EY.
Still exists? Yes.
Accessible? Yes.
Following cholera outbreaks in the mid-nineteenth century, sections of the New River around Stoke

Newington were piped underground. The redundant sections of the original watercourse were turned into ornamental waterways in a landscaped park.

Limehouse hydraulic accumulator tower

Location: Mill Place, Limehouse Basin, E14.

Still exists? Yes.

Accessible? Open occasionally (contact British Waterways); spiral staircase leads to a viewing gallery.

Mansell Street hydraulic accumulator tower

Location: Mansell Street, E1 (at south-east corner of railway bridge).

Still exists? Yes.

Accessible? No.

The Mansell Street accumulator – a typical example of its type. The faded lettering on the side of the tower proclaims 'London Midland & Scottish Railway City Goods Station and Bonded Stores' (photo taken in April 1975).

THE CRISP
THE CRISPIN
THE CRISP

New River Head

Location: 173 Rosebery Avenue, EC1R 4UN.
Still exists? Yes.
Accessible? Yes.
A small viewing area, enclosed by metal railings, overlooks the site of the New River Head but few historic features are visible. The site is still in operational use and one of the boreholes for the Thames Water Ring Main tunnel is located here. The former control building and headquarters of the Metropolitan Water Board has been converted into flats. Some features of New River Head can be viewed from Nautilus House Garden (accessible via Myddleton Passage).

OPPOSITE: Can you spot the characteristic accumulator tower in the background? It stood atop the Wilson Street warehouse, seen from Finsbury Avenue in April 1976.

Wapping hydraulic power station

Location: Wapping Wall, E1W 3SG.
Still exists? Yes.
Accessible? Open as a restaurant, bar, arts centre and exhibition space.

OXO
8
AGX 564
Reduced Camber
Asphalte or Wood
Concrete up to 1 ft. thick transmitting vibrations in entirety
Hydrant
Light Cable
48 in Water pumping Main to Reservoir
24 in Distribr Gas
36 in Gas distributing Main
Telephone Cables in earthenware ducts laid in Mortar in Concrete Conduit
Telephone Cables in Cast Iron Pipes
Cast Iron
Lead
Earthenware
9 in Water
old Cellar walled off when street widened
Brick and/or Concrete surface water sewer
P.O. Pneumatic
Telegram Carrier closed by rubber cap making air-tight fit: air pressure applied behind through vacuum in front
2 in Service
Telegraph
Power Cables
Telephone Cables
Telephone Cables
4 in Gas
6 in Hydraulic
30 in Water
36 in

Other underground utilities

SHARED SERVICE SUBWAYS

The notion of putting London's public utilities in subways or tunnels below ground first became reality in 1860. From this time onwards, shared service tunnels for gas and water pipes along with communications and power cables were an integral part of most progressive street improvements, such as Kingsway, Aldwych and Charing Cross Road together with the Victoria Embankment. During the twentieth century, they were also incorporated in development to create sub-surface booking halls at major tube stations, including Piccadilly Circus and Leicester Square.

Utility subways have the obvious advantage that there is no need to dig up the roadway every time alterations to services and new connections are needed. A further bonus is that faults and problems are less likely to occur because of the lack of disturbance. Shared use has its disadvantages too, as proved by a disastrous explosion at Holborn in 1928, when a gas leak ended up destroying many telephone cables.

OPPOSITE: Drawn in the 1930s, this illustration makes clear the kind of clutter that lies beneath our streets. As well as the gas, water and electricity mains, sewers and telephone cables, we can also see the slender tube of the pneumatic telegram 'pipeline' that survived into the 1960s.

Most of these subways are semicircular brick tunnels around 16 feet in diameter, which run about 3 feet below the pavement. Rectangular openings are provided at frequent intervals for access to the pipes and cables. In the past there have been hopes that all of these utility subways might be joined up end to end, but this has never occurred. Nevertheless, London currently has 9 miles of joint use service tunnels carrying water, electricity, gas, telephone wires and cable television (previously some also carried telegraph wires, hydraulic power conduits and pneumatic telegraph tubes).

Not all underground utility tunnels were shared, however, and some of the most interesting were bespoke constructions for exclusive use by their owners.

OPPOSITE: A section of Holborn Viaduct, showing cables and pipes beneath the pavement, plus sewers and the Pneumatic Despatch tube (see page 39) at a lower level.

LEFT: On the other hand, this 1863 drawing of the Euston Road near King's Cross station illustrates all too clearly how existing features like water mains, sewers and underground railways conspired to make utility subways an impossible dream in older streets.

ELECTRICAL INFRASTRUCTURE

For many years electricity substations of the smaller variety have been constructed underground, simply because there was no space available at surface level. On a completely different scale is the unique substation constructed entirely below ground beneath the gardens in the centre of Leicester Square. Both its power rating of 180MVA (effectively 180 million watts) and the volume it occupies 40 feet below ground are impressive, even if there is nothing to be seen by the observer at street level. It took two years to build, from 1989 to 1991, and when complete the gardens above it were fully landscaped to leave no trace of the construction works.

Most of the major electricity cable tunnels were built from 1990 onwards, made necessary by the greater use of electricity, with more offices using computers and air conditioning. The tunnels for these

Strict security was observed when the first strategic telephone cable tunnels were constructed under City streets in 1941 and this soldier's fixed bayonet is not just for show. His insignia indicate he is attached to the Home Guard, the COL on his shoulder standing for 'City of London' and 19 being his battalion number.

132kV cable routes are constructed using precast concrete linings, mostly of 8 feet 6 inches diameter. The longest of these runs 12 miles from Elstree to St John's Wood at up to 130 feet below London and its suburbs. Shorter tunnels include Pimlico and Wandsworth to Wimbledon (5½ miles), St John's Wood to Pakenham Street, WC1 (2¾ miles), Leicester Square to Duke Street near Grosvenor Square (1½ miles) and West Ham to North Greenwich (1 mile).

Although constructing cable tunnels is extremely expensive, once complete the tunnels negate the need for protracted duct digging at surface level in what is one of the world's busiest capital cities. The long-term benefits are obvious: disruption to residents, traffic and pedestrians is minimised; the risk of damage to cables by third parties is unlikely; maintenance is easier; and there is plenty of capacity for accommodating other cables.

TUNNELS FOR TELECOMS

The same argument applies to London's other tube network for cables. This belongs to BT (British Telecom) and comprises a network of mainly 7-foot-diameter steel-segment tunnels. Most of these were built during the four decades from the 1940s to the 1980s and today they run for a total of around 12 miles, mainly in central London but with two spurs reaching out towards the north-western and south-western suburbs. Links were also constructed into the Bakerloo and Central Line tunnels of the London Underground railways, whilst cables were also installed in several tube tunnels during the Second World War to provide greater route diversity in case of enemy bombing. There is a great similarity between

The equipment floors of Kingsway telephone exchange were constructed in full-size tube railway tunnels that were dug at the height of war. After the hostilities were over it was intended that these tunnels would enable express tube trains to bypass Chancery Lane station, anticipating the Crossrail scheme currently being planned.

these cable tunnels and the tubes of the London Underground, not only in the style of tunnelling but also in fascinating might-have-been projects that were cancelled in the austerity years of the early 1950s but would otherwise have doubled the extent of the system. Access to the network is mainly via shafts inside the adjacent exchanges, in exchange yards outside or, in a few cases, via staircases emerging into subways below the streets and pavements. Inside major exchanges large lifts carry cable drums and other equipment down to the tunnels around 100 feet below.

Also constructed underground was Kingsway trunk telephone exchange, built between 1950 and 1952 at Chancery Lane inside a former deep level air raid shelter (see next chapter for more about these). A government inquiry held after the war decided that the existing trunk telephone exchange at Faraday House, Blackfriars, was 'not in the best position nor, indeed, sufficiently protected for its important function'. To avoid serious disruption in any future conflict some of Faraday's cables should be diverted to another facility having more protection. Since this needed connection to the existing east–west cable tunnel, the only suitable location, according to the Ministry of Works, was the Chancery Lane deep tube shelter. Opened to traffic in 1954, Kingsway exchange played a major role for three decades in switching inland long-distance calls and later also became the London terminal of the first transatlantic telephone cable, as well as the mid-point of the 'Hot Line' between the USA and the Soviet Union presidents during the Cold War.

Its size was remarkable, with two parallel tunnels, each a quarter of a mile long and 16 feet wide, housing much of the equipment. Some three miles of racking were installed, carrying 337 miles of switchboard cable, along with a 1.5 megawatt generator for standby power generation. Little wonder that a newspaper report of 1968 described Kingsway as a 'telephone city under London'.

> A city under the city – that is Kingsway trunk exchange, 100 feet beneath the Holborn area of London. Fully self-contained, Kingsway could seal itself off from the rest of London – and its 200 Post Office staff could go on working there in comfort and safety. The exchange is air-conditioned, has its own water supply from an artesian well, and emergency power from four diesel generators. Fuel tanks hold 22,000 gallons – enough to keep the generators going for six weeks.

The 'underground town' description of Kingsway exchange was pretty accurate, what with its unique subterranean population and passageways named after the streets far above, together, with new names such as Third Avenue, By-Pass Alley and The Dog's Leg. Superseded by newer technologies, it now stands vacant, while BT attempts to find a new owner for this remarkable facility. Originally Kingsway and the deep level cable tunnels were highly secret, but a notable change of policy took place in 1967, when the tunnels were taken off the secret list and removed from the so-called 'D Notice' list of subjects prohibited from media coverage. The press were shown round various parts of the system and various illustrated features followed. British Pathé was so impressed that it took its newsreel cameras down below twice, screening views of the tunnels below the Post Office Tower in March 1967 and a visit to the caverns of Kingsway exchange in May 1968. Soon afterwards this policy of openness was reversed and these facilities became taboo once more until the peace dividend of the 1990s. Even now BT tends not to discuss the subject for security reasons.

THE POST OFFICE RAILWAY AND ITS PREDECESSORS

Following a number of demonstrations of underground railways for transporting the mail in London, the first line was opened in 1863, connecting Euston railway station with the nearby North West District sorting office. It used 2-foot gauge track and air pressure to propel trucks through a more or less airtight tunnel. This was followed by a longer, 3 foot 8½-inch gauge line also from Euston, reaching Holborn in 1865 and the General Post Office at St Martin's-le-Grand in 1873.

Ingenious as this was, the service shaved only four minutes off the time taken to carry the mail by road and in 1874 the line was abandoned. The terminus at the General Post Office became a coal and wood store, whilst other parts of the 5-foot cast-iron

horseshoe-shaped tunnel were put to other uses. In 1895 there was a proposal to reopen the tunnel with electric traction and a new company was formed. Some work was done on upgrading the line and tunnels, but the Post Office remained sceptical about its worth. Work on the new project ceased in 1902 and the London Despatch Company was wound up in 1905. The Post Office finally bought the tunnel in 1921 to use for telephone cables, after which time it became known as 'the old parcels tube'. Several sections of the tunnel have been lost over the years but about three quarters of it is still in use, carrying cables. On 20 June 1928 an explosion in the tunnel under High Holborn was blamed on the ignition of

The Pneumatic Despatch, opened in 1865, was the first underground railway for mail traffic in London. Air pressure was used to blow the trains through the tunnels, in peashooter fashion.

coal gas, with one workman killed. During the subsequent excavations to repair half a mile of damaged road, four of the original mailbag cars were discovered (but not, unfortunately, preserved).

By 1900 traffic congestion on London's streets was becoming sufficiently acute to warrant reconsideration of a dedicated tube railway for carrying the mail, using electric trains on 2-foot-gauge track in 9-foot-diameter tunnels, 70 feet below the streets of London. After due consideration it was decided in 1911 to construct this double track tube railway, connecting two main line railway stations and several sorting offices along a 6-mile east–west axis from Whitechapel to Paddington. Construction took much longer than expected; tunnel boring began in 1915 but shortage of labour and materials under wartime conditions caused slow progress. Track laying began finally in 1924 and the railway did not open to operational traffic until 1928.

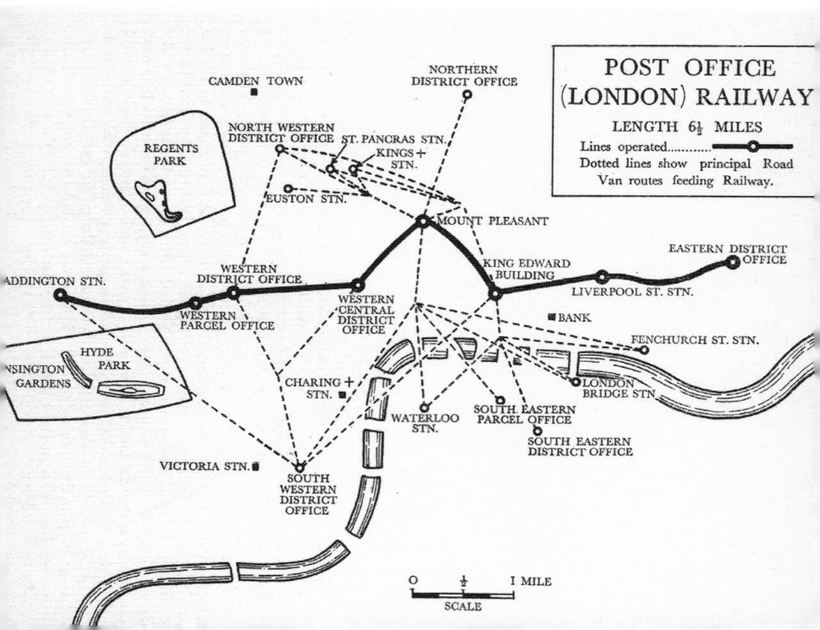

A plan of the Post Office Railway. Extensions were planned to King's Cross, Euston, Waterloo, Cannon Street and London Bridge main line stations, but were never built.

As well as carrying up to 4 million letters a day, the Post Office Railway handled construction materials in 1941–2 when cable tunnels were being constructed in the City of London.

Once operational the railway was a resounding success. At its height it was carrying an average of 4 million letters every day between the nine stations along the route, operating 19 hours a day for 286 days a year. The driverless trains were operated automatically, latterly under computer control, on the journey from Paddington to Whitechapel, which with all stops took 26 minutes. For all this the Post Office Railway, also branded Mail Rail, was constrained by an inherent inflexibility that led Royal Mail to announce its closure, which took place on 30 May 2003. Letter mail no longer came into London by train and the restructuring of London's postal service meant that many of the sorting offices served by Mail Rail had been replaced by vast new mail centres located in the suburbs. David Chapman, Royal Mail's London Programme Manager, said:

> Mail Rail has played a vital part in delivering the capital's daily postbag over the past 75 years and we appreciate that. However, it is well past its prime. We understand … the potential it offers for other uses.

> We want to talk to businesses with commercial propositions, as well as our unions, about how the trains, tunnels or tracks might be used, and are already in discussions with a couple of organisations. We would like to hear from heritage and other groups that might have realistic proposals.

At the time of writing the line is mothballed and no firm proposals have been published for its future.

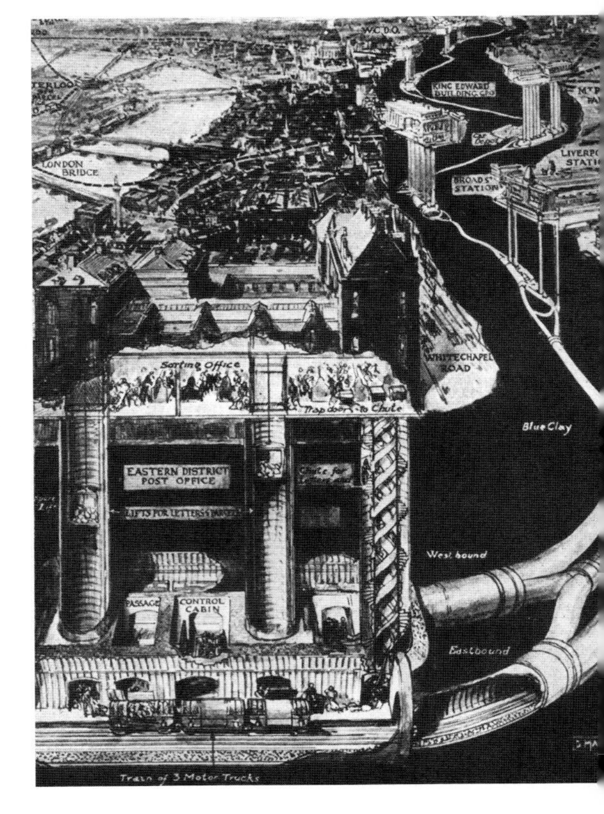

This striking illustration of the Post Office Railway appeared in *The Graphic*. In the foreground is the Eastern District Office in Whitechapel, with the railway snaking its way to Paddington station in the far distance.

TUNNELS FOR TRAVELLERS

To include underground passenger facilities would have doubled the size of this book, so instead they are to be covered in a companion volume.

PLACES TO VISIT

Kingsway 'secret' telephone exchange

Location: 31–33 High Holborn, WC1V 6AX.
Still exists? Yes.
Accessible? No access to interior.
The scruffy double doors gave access to a hallway and staircase that led to the basement level, where a lift took staff down to the vast telephone exchange housed in two tube tunnels. The massive goods entrance is not far away at 39 Furnival Street, EC4A 1JQ.

Leicester Square electricity substation

Location: The Lodge, Leicester Square Gardens, WC2H 7NJ.
Still exists? Yes.
Accessible? No access to interior.
The only external evidence for this massive facility is the Ticketmaster ticket booth, which surrounds an unseen ventilation shaft.

For nearly forty years the inconspicuous double doors at the centre of this photograph led down to a vast trunk telephone exchange 100 feet below ground. This building (but not the tunnels below) has been sold to a property developer.

SHELTER
S
HERE

Protecting people, production and government

AIR RAID SHELTERS FOR CIVILIANS

Providing secure shelter for the population under bombardment is a nightmare scenario, simply because 100 per cent protection would be impossible without limitless finance and resources. During the Second World War shelter was provided in a number of ways – by providing 'do it yourself' Anderson and Morrison shelters for individual families, reinforced communal shelters in streets (above ground), small local sub-surface shelters in parks, schools and other public buildings and some mass underground shelters, either in tube stations and tunnels or in purpose-built constructions. Of these, the high-capacity 'civilian deep shelters' are by far the most impressive and significant.

During the 1930s some of London's tube railways were suffering extreme overcrowding during peak hours and four senior London Transport staff made a visit to New York to investigate how the subways there coped with similar problems. One of the solutions they came up with was a scheme for building relief lines that would enable express Tube

OPPOSITE: Conspicuous signs marked the entrance to air raid shelters during the Second World War. This is the north side of Russell Square, with Southampton Row and the Hotel Russell in the background.

A large white 'S' on a black background distinguished these signs from others. Shades minimised any light spill that might be seen by bombers overhead. In any case blackout regulations meant their illumination was by a single 15-watt bulb, even though they were designed to be visible at a distance of 100 feet.

trains to bypass the less-used stations, with proposals drawn up for the Northern, Central and Bakerloo lines. Although soon deferred, these plans were dusted off again when locations were sought by the Ministry of Home Security for deep shelters to protect civilians in London in November 1940. Plans were examined for ten twin parallel tube tunnels of 16 foot 6 inch diameter and 400 yards long that would accommodate 9,600 persons in bunks. These new trains would be placed below existing station tunnels at places where the deep-level express tubes would not stop (it would not be possible to re-use the shelter tubes for stations as the tunnel diameter was too small). The locations nominated for the north of the River Thames were Belsize Park, Camden Town, Chancery Lane, Goodge Street and St Paul's (later abandoned). South of the Thames, the nominated locations were Clapham Common, Clapham North, Clapham South, Oval (later abandoned), and Stockwell.

Two of these structures were abandoned at an early stage. At Oval construction was halted because water ingress was so persistent that it would have made further construction prohibitively expensive. At St Paul's the cathedral authorities objected that the tunnelling might damage the foundations of the cathedral.

The first use of these shelters was in 1943, for billeting troops on leave; occupation by civilians did not begin until mid-1944. Even then, some of the

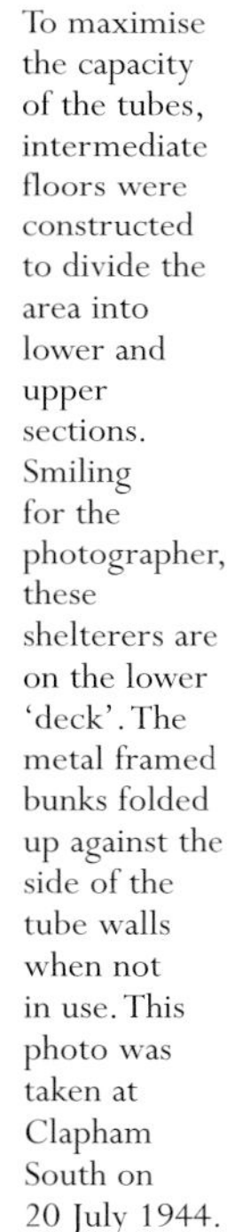

To maximise the capacity of the tubes, intermediate floors were constructed to divide the area into lower and upper sections. Smiling for the photographer, these shelterers are on the lower 'deck'. The metal framed bunks folded up against the side of the tube walls when not in use. This photo was taken at Clapham South on 20 July 1944.

By some miracle all the wartime bunks have survived intact on both sides of this tunnel at Camden Town.

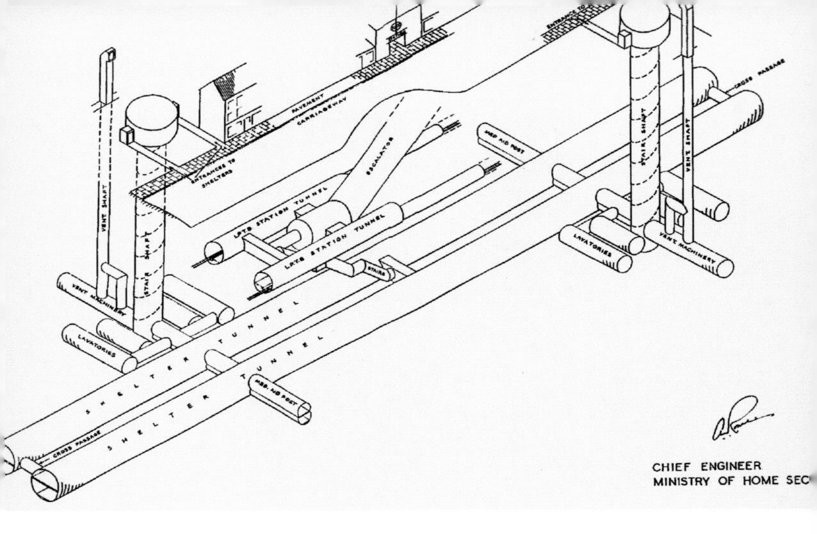

This diagram shows the way the tubes were divided into two levels. First Aid posts, toilets, communal washing areas and ventilation equipment were placed in side tunnels. Also visible are the air shafts and the lift shafts surrounded by spiral staircases, as well as the emergency exit to the platforms of the adjacent tube station.

shelters were retained for government purposes. Camden Town was used as a hostel for troops from 1943 to 1947. Chancery Lane was equipped as working and sleeping accommodation for key government staff, and also used as a military hostel and later by security services (subsequently it was opened as Kingsway telephone exchange in 1954, being used for storage only from 1990 onwards). Clapham Common was used during the war as a hostel for American troops. Clapham South was used as weekend troop accommodation from 1943 during the war and afterwards, as a leave hostel from June 1945, and as armed forces troop billets in 1946. In addition it was used as a hostel for Jamaican immigrants in 1948, as the Festival Hotel for provincial visitors to London in 1951, as a troop billet for the funeral of King George VI in 1952 and finally as accommodation for Coronation visitors in 1953. Goodge Street was used by US and British forces from 1943 to 1945 and as an armed forces hostel from 1947 until a disastrous fire in 1956.

Stockwell was used by British and US troops as a hostel during the war, as a leave hostel from 1945 and then for museum and record storage from 1947 until May 1951.

OTHER TUNNEL SHELTERS

Admirable as these purpose-built shelters were, they were of use only to people in specific parts of London. The authorities were under extreme pressure to do something for the densely populated East End of London, where use was made of brand new tunnels that had been constructed for the eastern extension of the Central Line of the London Underground. Work on this project had ceased in May 1940, leaving trackless tunnels that were fairly suitable, if not ideal, for use as shelters. By August of the same year a shelter for 2,500 people (complete with a canteen) had opened just east of Liverpool Street station and another at the unfinished Bethnal Green tube station. This was later the location of the worst single civilian death toll of the Second World War. The site is marked today by a blue plaque memorial, which states that on Wednesday 3 March 1943 some 173 panicking men, women and children died as they were descending the steps of the official station entrance to seek shelter. Further east, the entire ¾-mile stretch of tunnel between Stratford and Leyton station became an air raid shelter, as did two tube tunnel bores for a distance of 350 feet north-east of the Gainsborough Road tunnel portal at Leytonstone. None of these tunnel shelters was ideal: toilet provision was abominable, there was theft and vandalism and conditions in general were distinctly uncomfortable and unpleasant.

Further east along what was to become the Central Line, a shelter was initially opened at the future Redbridge station but this was soon afterwards assigned to factory production of war supplies (see below). The protection that it offered was mainly psychological, probably less than the Morrison and Anderson shelters that its users had forsaken, simply because it was only just below ground level. In fact the station was built so close to the surface that no escalators were required to reach the station platforms. Another shelter 'out east' was opened in the public pedestrian subways of the future Gants Hill station, using the six roadside staircases that are still in use today as station entrances.

GOVERNMENT BUNKERS AND BOLT-HOLES

The government also constructed a number of bomb-proof and gas-proof citadels for maintaining what it called its 'due functioning' or continued operation. One of the most substantial was located beside Horseferry Road, where a complex of three protected facilities known as the North and South Rotundas and the Horseferry Road Citadel were built on the site of an old gasworks. By creating hardened accommodation (a rectangular blockhouse and two circular bunkers built in old gasholder pits) they were able to duplicate Air Ministry premises in Whitehall, to which they were linked by tunnel. These works were not demolished until 2003, when explosives had to be used because 'all the drills are bouncing off the three-foot-thick wall', according to a newspaper report.

Another massive construction was the Cabinet War Rooms, located beneath existing government offices

fronting on Storey's Gate, Great George Street and King Charles Street. Started in 1938, it became fully operational on 27 August 1939, precisely one week before the outbreak of war. For the next six years this became the hub of government, where 400 staff collected and processed information about all aspects of the national and world situation, to brief the decision-makers and then disseminate those decisions. Although plans were made to hold Cabinet meetings at the Paddock bunker at Dollis Hill and in the basement of the North Rotunda, Churchill asserted that he personally had no intention of moving unless London suffered a scale of attack far worse than anything experienced to that time. The Cabinet War Rooms is probably the best known of all the subterranean constructions completed during the Second World War and a far-sighted decision was made in 1949 to preserve it intact as a memorial of the war. It took another thirty-five years before it was opened to public inspection, however, and it is now one of London's major tourist attractions.

Provision for due functioning, old and new: the wartime Rotunda citadel and 1960s government offices at Monck Street, London SW1. Both structures have now been demolished.

A vast amount of time and dedicated effort has gone into finding the correct 1940s period paraphernalia to restore the Cabinet War Rooms beneath Whitehall. It's little wonder that this is now one of London's most popular visitor attractions.

In 1941 the government built a number of strong steel-framed buildings in central London and four 'fortresses', which came to be popularly known as 'citadels'. The War Office citadel in Whitehall, also known as 'The Fortress', was built beneath the Montagu House annexe and had a subway connection to the basement of the War Office. The much better known Admiralty citadel was built as a two-storey above-ground bunker to provide bomb-proof protection for the vital Admiralty operations, wireless and communications rooms. During the Second World War it functioned as a huge nerve centre through which signals passed from all over the world, and even today press visits are not permitted. Its foundations are stated to be 30 feet deep and the concrete roof 20 feet thick. Grass on the roof of the building provides a degree of camouflage, whilst another fascinating feature is the machine gun slits at each corner of the building (to cover enemies attacking from the Park or the Mall).

Other less well-known citadel structures of the Second World War were the Kensington, Mayfair and Faraday citadels. The first of these, also known as the South Kensington Blockhouse, was London's civil defence headquarters. A single-storey surface bunker of reinforced concrete with 6-foot-thick walls, it was built next to the Geological Museum (now part of the Natural History Museum) close to the junction of Exhibition Road and Cromwell Road in South Kensington. It is still used by the museum. The 'bomb-proof Curzon Street building' known as the Mayfair citadel was the sole example in London of a bunker and office block constructed as a single unit. Erected in 1939, it was intended for use as Home Forces General Headquarters and reportedly it was also made available for the use of the Royal Family should Buckingham Palace be bombed. In fact, it was used purely as office accommodation, partly because, being some distance from Whitehall and not connected by tunnel, it was unsuitable for strategic protection.

The Faraday citadel, another of the structures started in 1941, was part of the main trunk telephone exchange at Godliman Street just south of St Paul's Cathedral. Into this building went 40,000 tons of concrete, 2,200 tons of reinforced steel, and onto it went a concrete roof 7 feet 6 inches thick. It was completely self-contained, with its own continuous water supply, enough food for three months, and sleeping accommodation for off-duty personnel. Built and used primarily as a telephone exchange, a government report of 1943 stated, '[it] has a high degree of protection but is not bombproof. It is furnished for Cabinet Ministers but is inconveniently situated.' It remained in use for its main purpose until 1989, after which it was demolished.

NEW ROLES FOR DISUSED TUBE STATIONS

During the Second World War several disused tube stations were pressed into use for a variety of purposes. British Museum station on the Central Line (closed in 1933 when it was replaced by Holborn Kingsway) was opened in 1941 as a public air raid shelter for 625 people. Brompton Road on the Piccadilly line closed in 1934 and its lift shafts and platform-level accommodation were used throughout the war by the 1st Anti-Aircraft Division for controlling the anti-aircraft guns defending London. Staff here received details of enemy air raids by telephone from the Royal Air Force radar chain via RAF Uxbridge and plotted the raids on map tables so that the commanders in the gallery could view the enemy numbers and flight paths. Orders were then sent to the numerous gun sites in order to destroy the enemy's aircraft.

Disused areas of another Piccadilly Line station, Green Park, played a wartime role. A passageway at the Dover Street entrance to the station was used for storing valuables of the London Museum, whilst plans were made in 1940 for the Prime Minister's bedroom, bathroom/toilet, a private office, a secretary's office and a conference room. In fact this location was abandoned in favour of the nearby closed station of Down Street, after which the area was fitted out as an emergency bolt-hole for the chairman and twenty-five departmental heads of

London Transport. Similar emergency offices for the three operating managers and their staff were built on the disused Aldwych branch platform at Holborn. Down Street station, disused since 1932, had its platforms walled off and meeting rooms, kitchens, dormitories and other facilities provided by partitioning the space remaining on the platforms. Further offices, meeting rooms and a typing pool were provided in the low-level subway leading to the platforms from the lift shaft, with gas-proof doors provided at appropriate points. This was used as the protected headquarters of the Railway Executive Committee, a collaborative effort of the main line railway companies that coordinated train movements between the different systems. At extremely short notice arrangements had to be made for moving men, guns and ammunition from one part of the country to another. During the D-Day invasion period more than seventy ambulance trains were run each week, and as late as 1946 the control room was still having to arrange for more than 2,500 special trains in a period of seven days.

One section of the offices at Down Street was built specially for the use of Churchill and the War Cabinet. Frequent use of this 'underground hive of industry' was made by Churchill and his ministers whenever necessary. Both Churchill and his wife used the place as alternative sleeping quarters from 1941 to 1943. During the bombing Mrs Churchill would sometimes emerge onto the platform and travel by Tube train to various stations to make surprise visits to people sheltering on the platforms. Finally, as discussed briefly in the last chapter of this book, the original entrance to St Paul's station on the Central Line (originally called Post Office) was also revived for war purposes, becoming the national control centre for Britain's electricity grid.

FANTASTIC FACTORY

Factories went underground too and during the Second World War some massive production facilities were constructed, mainly for the aircraft industry, in the West Midlands and near Corsham in Wiltshire. Just east of London what was described as a 'fantastic factory' in tunnels built (but not yet completed) for an extension of the Underground's Central Line from Liverpool Street to Epping. In twin tunnels just under 2½ miles long, the production facilities occupied 300,000 square feet of floor space and employed a total of 2,000 workers (mainly female). The Plessey company was the occupier of these facilities, which became the most successful underground factory in the country. Production here included wiring looms

The great extent of the underground Plessey factory in Essex is seen in this imaginative collage. A minor error is that Redbridge, which is London's shallowest tube station, has never had escalators.

With Plessey's underground factory stretching two and a half miles, intermediate entry points were constructed along Eastern Avenue to make it easier for staff to reach their workplace. Equipped with lifts, these shafts still survive and stand out starkly between the suburban houses.

for Halifax and Lancaster bombers, a quarter of a million aircraft pumps, wireless equipment, 22,000 cartridge starters for fighters, gear levers for armoured vehicles, shell fuses and field telephones.

Observers describe this strange workplace as a brightly lit and unending circular tunnel with on one side a long single row of machines tended by young ladies in white overalls and on the other side an 18-inch-gauge railway track carrying 'a very serviceable train on its endless journey of fetch and carry'. Its work done, the factory closed in 1945, after which it took five months to remove the factory plant plus another seven to break up and remove the concrete false floor, air conditioning and other

At Redbridge station, wall displays tell the story of London's secret wartime factory. Until Norman Gunby instigated a project to erect these historical plaques, few of today's passengers were aware of the vital role that Wanstead, Redbridge and Gants Hill stations once played.

paraphernalia. In all some 12,000 tons of equipment and concrete had to be removed before track laying could commence for the new Tube trains that first ran in December 1947. Needless to say, discussion of the factory and its working was forbidden during the war and entry was by production of a pass only. Not until 1946 was any public announcement made of what went on underground and little mention was made again until 1985, when the Plessey Company made major publicity of its wartime secret.

PLACES TO VISIT

Admiralty citadel

Location: Corner of The Mall and Horse Guards Parade, SW1A.

Still exists? Yes.

Accessible? No access to interior but visitors can walk past three sides of the structure.

Cabinet War Rooms and Churchill Museum

Location: Clive Steps, King Charles Street, SW1A 2AQ.

Still exists? Yes.

Accessible? Yes (open daily except 24, 25 and 26 December).

Visitors can walk past the Map Room, the Cabinet Room and Churchill's bedroom, all restored faithfully using authentic period fittings and furniture.

Civilian deep shelter surface buildings

Locations: Belsize Park (corner of Haverstock Hill and Downside Crescent); Camden Town (Buck Street, NW1 and Underhill Street, NW1 behind Marks and Spencer car park); Clapham Common (junction of Clapham High Street and Clapham Park Road, SW4); Clapham North (400 Clapham Road SW4, on the west side opposite 383 Clapham Road); Clapham South (junction of Clapham Common South Side, Nightingale Lane and The Avenue, SW4); Goodge Street (junction of Chenies Street and North Crescent, WC1, and Tottenham Court Road, WC1 west side, adjoining the American Church and opposite junction with Torrington Place (north)); Stockwell (island at junction of South Lambeth Road and Clapham Road, SW9).

Still exists? Yes.

Accessible? No access to interiors. Entrances not listed are not on or near public property.

At surface level strange 'shafthead' buildings provided access to deep shelters, built massively in a style that must have looked very modernistic in the 1940s. This is the Chenies Street entrance to the Goodge Street deep shelter in the centre of London, which during the war was used by General Eisenhower as his military control centre and is today a secure storage area for commercial documents and digital data.

Eastern Avenue

Location: Eastern Avenue, Ilford, IG4 5AB on south side opposite junction with Danehurst Gardens.
Still exists? Yes.
Accessible? No access to interior.
This shaft provided access to the wartime Plessey factory below. It is now an air vent and emergency access point for the Central Line of the London Underground. Another shaft still emerges in the middle of the roundabout at Redbridge, where the new North Circular Road crosses Eastern Avenue. This shaft provides access to the pump room underground.

Kensington citadel

Location: Junction of Exhibition Road, SW7 5BD and Cromwell Road.
Still exists? Yes, as part of the Natural History Museum.
Accessible? No access to interior but clearly visible from the west side of Exhibition Road.
This structure remains in use by the Natural History Museum's palaeontology department for storage and

The same location in 1957, before this and other deep shelter entrance buildings underwent a 'beautification' programme. This involved reducing the height of wooden vent stacks and removing ugly metal pipework.

vibration-free microscopy work. A plant room serving the whole museum is also here.

London Transport staff making aircraft parts at Earl's Court on 10 September 1942 in a subway that had been closed for the duration of the war.

Redbridge station

Location: Redbridge Lane East, Wanstead, IG4 5BG.
Still exists? Yes.
Accessible? Yes.
Wall displays at platform level tell the story of London's secret wartime factory erected in the tube train tunnels here.

The odd

THIS FINAL CHAPTER covers a selection of unusual and amusing items that didn't fit elsewhere in the book but seemed far too interesting to omit.

Sewer gas lamps

Location: Carting Lane, WC2R.
Still exists? Yes.
Accessible? Yes, public thoroughfare.
Considering the 'cargo' that sewers carry, it is hardly surprising that offensive pockets of biogas (mainly methane and hydrogen sulphide) can build up. Methane is explosive and if not released, this gas can leak out, causing unpleasant odours. In some districts tall iron pipes (also known as stench pipes) were erected in streets to vent sewers, and some of these were quite ornate. One of the finest inventions of the nineteenth century was the Sewer Gas Destructor Lamp, patented in 1895 by Joseph Webb of Birmingham. The inventor's solution was to allow sewer gas to vent into the hot flame on an ordinary gas street lamp, and a number of his lamps were installed in London and other cities. One survived in

OPPOSITE: London's last sewer gas destructor lamp stands in Carting Lane, near the Savoy Hotel between the Strand and the Embankment.

Not all sewer vent pipes are as ornamental as this example photographed in May 1978 at Carshalton in the London Borough of Sutton. The 'portholes' are covered with wire netting to stop birds nesting.

Dansey Yard, Soho into the early 1960s and the very last example can be found in Carting Lane, just off the Strand.

Underground restaurant

Location: St Paul's Churchyard (south side), EC4M.
Still exists? No.
Accessible? No.
In 1900 the *Harmsworth Magazine* described this remarkable eating place:

> On our way we pass through St Paul's Churchyard, and are struck by a circular glass structure in the middle of the roadway on the south-east side. This proves on investigation to be nothing else than the roof of an underground restaurant, belonging to the British Tea Table Limited. No entrance is visible, but in Old Change we find a doorway by which we obtain access to a long passage running under a row of warehouses and leading to the restaurant under St Paul's Churchyard. The interior is a surprise, for the glass roof makes it as light as day, but the numerous alcoves and side rooms are in Cimmerian darkness until the electric light is turned on. There are plenty of basement restaurants in London, but we know of no other example under the middle of a road.

The glass roof of the restaurant was constructed below a street island in the middle of the road junction where St Paul's Churchyard ends and Cannon Street starts. This is visible on old street plans. Incidentally, this restaurant should not be confused with the underground 'tea-rooms' of pre-war London mentioned by Michael Harrison in

London's highly unusual underground restaurant at St Paul's was connected to its street entrance by a tunnel, from which two guests are seen emerging.

his excellent book, *London Beneath The Pavement*. These tea-rooms were just cellars fitted out to serve drinks rather more spiritual than tea. One ended up being closed down after a country housewife entered a respectable-looking cellar tea-room, intent upon a refreshing cup of tea. Harrison relates, 'She asked for it and got it. But the foolish waitress could not discriminate between the housewife and her regular customers, and insisted that the lady pay the usual five shillings, which ordinarily purchased more than a solitary cup of tea.' The upshot was that after the lady left, she collared the first policeman she saw and insisted he investigate the reason for this daylight robbery.

South Kensington museums subway

Location: Runs from South Kensington station to museums in Exhibition Road SW7.

Still exists? Yes.

Accessible? Yes.

In the centre of this road island is the circular glass roof of London's decidedly unusual underground restaurant. It was lit by 'electric light', which must have been a novelty compared with the more general gas illumination of the time.

The crowds who use the 484-yard covered way from South Kensington underground station leading to the museums may well be unaware of its long history. Constructed in 1885 by the Metropolitan District Railway Company (the forerunner of today's District Line), it was provided to enable passengers to reach the grounds of the newly opened Inventions Exhibition under cover. In those days passengers using the tunnel paid a penny one way or 1½d there and back. Apparently the subway closed after the Colonial and Indian Exhibition ended in 1886, but reopened again permanently in December 1908, when it became free of charge. To the observant eye the remains of the ticket offices were still visible at each end of the subway until about 1970, when the southern office became a shop unit and the northern ticket window was stopped up.

Still in constant use, the roomy subway is faced in pale glazed bricks and its arched roof contains substantial riveted steelwork. There are entrances to the Science Museum, the Ismaili Centre, the Natural History Museum, Imperial College, and the Royal College of Music, and according to the South Kensington Underground Development Action Group's website, more than 50 million journeys are made along the subway every year.

Stories that the tunnel once ran as far as the Royal Albert Hall are unfounded, although at one time there was a covered arcade from where the present subway stops to the Hall. An extension of the subway was kept in mind for some years, and it is understood that the college buildings on the west side of Exhibition Road were built with clearances to accommodate such a subway.

Some may disagree with blogger Frankie Roberto, who considers the pedestrian subway under Exhibition Road one of the world's worst urban spaces. At most times, he says, it's a soulless, never-ending tunnel of despair, with little daylight, and prone to leaking when it rains.

Post Office Telegraph's street tube network

Location: Large network covering much of inner London.

Still exists? Disused.

Accessible? No.

Today's traffic congestion in London was easily matched by conditions in the later nineteenth century, which made it ironic that a telegram could be sent in a matter of minutes but could then take an hour or more to be delivered. The solution was the pneumatic tube carrier, in which messages were carried in felt bags sucked by air pressure along 1½-inch-diameter metal tubes under the pavements of London. Following the first installation in 1853 a large network grew up to embrace at its peak some 57 miles of pipeline reaching branch offices all over the capital.

The network itself radiated from the Central Telegraph Office in Newgate Street EC2, on the same site where British Telecom's head office building

Artist's sketch of the pneumatic tube station in the basement of the Central Telegraph Office in Newgate Street. Telegraph clerks sorted 'pneumagrams' and handed these to operators who sent them on their way to the delivery office by compressed air.

stands now. The CTO, as it was generally called, suffered considerable bomb damage during the Second World War. Despite this, the street tube network was not abandoned, but was repaired and maintained in just about full operation until 1962, when the more prevalent use of telex and the telephone made further investment in the telegram system unviable.

Gordon's Wine Bar – a watering hole that had no licence

Location: 47 Villiers Street, WC2N 6NE.
Still exists? Yes.
Accessible? Yes, during opening hours.
Within two minutes' walk of Charing Cross station is a small and unobtrusive wine house that does a thriving trade yet until 2006 had never had a licence. In the year 1364, King Edward III granted Royal Letters Patent to the 'Mistery of the Vintners'. As a result, these merchants were allowed to open premises and sell wine without applying for a licence. This quaint anomaly, known as the Vintners' Privilege, finally came to an end as a result of licensing law changes made in 2003.

Gordon's was established in its present form in 1890 by Arthur Gordon, who was one of the few remaining 'free vintners' able to set up and sell wine anywhere without applying for a licence. Claiming to be the

A somewhat grainy image taken from an old price card issued by Gordon's Wine Bar. The establishment does a thriving trade, yet never held a licence.

oldest wine bar in London, it occupies a small cellar beneath what was once Samuel Pepys's house. The bar has not changed in decades, with old wooden walls covered in historical newspaper cuttings and memorabilia faded with age. For many years it operated without any sign to announce its existence and was something of a secret given only to those in the know. Nowadays its website ensures it gains far wider recognition.

The BBC Stronghold and other underground studios

Location: Immediately north of Broadcasting House, 2–22 Portland Place, W1A 1AA.
Still exists? No.
Accessible? No.
Although the BBC endeavoured to evacuate as many of its staff as possible away from the risk of bombing during the Second World War, many staff had to remain in London. Several studios were constructed below ground, the largest of which was a 'complete

The Stronghold is the name given by the BBC to a complete broadcasting centre in miniature that was constructed just north of Broadcasting House during the Second World War. Its concrete roof was 9 feet 6 inches thick.

broadcasting station in miniature' built at the rear of Broadcasting House.

Known as 'The Stronghold', it was not revealed to the public at large until 1946. The underground structure contained studios, recording rooms, a control room, offices and a small canteen, all protected by a concrete roof 9 feet 6 inches thick. Completed in November 1942, the Stronghold was intended for emergency use only and in fact it was never needed, although the main Broadcasting House was bombed on several occasions.

Some 10,000 tons of concrete were used to construct the Stronghold, which was designed from the outset to form part of a subsequent extension to Broadcasting House. In the event this did not come to pass and the Stronghold was demolished in 2008 when the new extension was finally built. Other wartime underground studios in London were established at 200 Oxford Street (deep underneath the Peter Robinson department store), under the Criterion Theatre (Piccadilly Circus), the Paris and Monseigneur news theatres (Waterloo Place at the bottom of Lower Regent Street and Marble Arch respectively) and at Bush House (Aldwych). Emergency news studios were created beneath a private residence named Kelvedon in Woodside Avenue, Finchley, N12, and in the basement of a block of flats in Grosvenor Square, diagonally across the square from the American Embassy.

Churchill's decoy toilet

Location: Cabinet War Rooms, Clive Steps, King Charles Street, SW1A 2AQ.

Still exists? Yes.

Accessible? Yes.

'The loo that wasn't' was one of the best cover stories of the Second World War. This innocent door in the Cabinet War Rooms beneath Whitehall led not to a lavatory but to a secret room used for transatlantic radio-telephone calls by Churchill alone. The vacant/engaged indicator on the door ensured that nobody would disturb the very special occupant.

One of the best kept secrets of the Second World War is the secret transatlantic telephone system that enabled Churchill to speak to the President of the United States in total confidence from his bunker in the Cabinet War Rooms beneath Whitehall. What makes this even more remarkable are the digital cryptography techniques employed that made this in fact the first unbreakable online speech coding system.

The intense secrecy of this vital communication link was maintained by disguising the soundproofed cubicle in which Churchill held his covert conversations with President Roosevelt in Washington as a lavatory. Nobody would ever disturb this meeting of minds because the door was provided with a standard toilet lock and indicator; to all and sundry it was merely Churchill's executive loo. The Cabinet War Rooms have been restored to their wartime state as a museum and today 'the loo that wasn't' can be seen by any visitor to the Churchill Museum and Cabinet War Rooms.

The London Silver Vaults

Location: Chancery House, 53–64 Chancery Lane, WC2A 1QT.

Still exists? Yes.

Accessible? Yes (shopping hours).

Traditionally many of London's specialist trades have stored their wares underground. A century ago it was said that there were 28 miles of subterranean wine vaults in London. One such subterranean storeroom that everyone can visit is the London Silver Vaults, a collection of forty shops said to contain the largest

The London Silver Vaults, today a specialist retail complex, was originally known as the Chancery Lane Safe Deposit. The company boasted of 6,000 safes immovably fixed in strong rooms for private use, guarded night and day by military patrols. This photo, taken around 1905, shows some of the deposit boxes used by individuals.

display of silver under one roof in the world. As well as silver you can also buy (or admire) high-class jewellery and *objets d'art*. The vaults are on the site of the Chancery Lane Safe Deposit, which opened in 1876 to provide strong rooms to people who needed to safeguard their household silver, jewellery and personal documents. Over the years the vaults were also used by silver dealers who required secure storage for their valuable stock and the now world renowned London Silver Vaults opened in its present form in 1953.

The disused lift shafts that became the nerve centre of the country's electricity transmission network (1940–5)

Location: Beneath western corner of Newgate Street and King Edward Street, EC1A.

Still exists? Disused.

Accessible? No.

Air attacks on the Central Electricity Board's grid control centre next to Bankside power station (now the Tate Modern) forced it to find safer premises underground. The location selected was the disused lift shafts of St Paul's underground station, into which a new entrance with escalators had been constructed in January 1939. The two lift shafts that were no longer needed were lined with 18 inches of reinforced concrete as protection against bombs penetrating diagonally and for supporting floors of the same thickness. The result was a totally protected national control centre 120 feet deep, with thirteen separate rooms equipped with mosaic diagrams, feeder loading diagrams with indicating meters and communication by telephone and teleprinter, with area control centres at Glasgow, Newcastle, Manchester, Leeds, Birmingham and Bristol. A replacement control centre opened above ground nearby in 1950 but the equipment room remained behind, much to the disgust of the telecomms technicians who still had to cross Newgate Street and descend below ground. This remained the case until 1957 when both Paternoster Control (on the surface) and St Paul's (in 'The Hole') closed altogether.

An underground recording studio owned by the Post Office

Location: Brook Road, NW2 7DZ.
Still exists? Yes.
Accessible? Yes, once a year on London Open House Day.

More by accident than by design, the British Post Office became involved in many strange activities during the Second World War. Its work with the Colossus, Cobra and Tunney computer devices for breaking enemy codes at Bletchley Park is now fairly well known, whereas similar work producing high-speed computers for co-ordinating anti-aircraft gunnery and for timing bomb release has not

This was the national control room for Britain's electricity supply from 1941 to 1950 – crammed along with substantial equipment racks into a 120-foot-deep circular lift shaft at St Paul's tube station! Seen here are the instrument panel with recording meters below, the frequency meter (showing 50Hz) and the National Grid diagram.

received the same recognition. All these were designed at the Post Office research station at Dollis Hill, where a totally bomb-proof subterranean war citadel was built 40 feet below ground. Intended for use by Churchill's War Cabinet, it was fitted out with a Map Room, Cabinet Room and offices, all housed within a sub-basement protected by a 5-foot-thick concrete roof.

It was in this underground bunker that a special chamber was constructed to simulate an infantry tank's interior for training the radio operators who had to send and receive messages under deafening conditions. Producing the sound effects was problematic; recordings on 78rpm gramophone records would not last long enough and instead recordings of a tank rumbling past a microphone were played continuously on a speaking clock machine.

Similar machines were made for the Royal Air Force; these generated continuous background aircraft noise effects for training radio operators. Four different aircraft types were covered, at normal speed and at absolute maximum. Yet another machine

The location codenamed Paddock, where sound effects for military training were recorded 40 feet below ground, was a well-kept secret during the Second World War. Revealed four decades later to lie beneath the Post Office research station at Dollis Hill in north-west London, the rather dilapidated accom-modation is now open to intrepid visitors once or twice a year.

was for training fighter pilots; this was a twin-channel simulator, providing continuous aircraft noise and spasmodic machine-gun effects as and when required.

Safe refuges for national treasures during the Second World War

Location: Piccadilly Circus and Aldwych underground stations.
Still exists? Yes.
Accessible? Former storage areas are off-limits.
The oft-expressed notion that Britain 'sleepwalked' into the Second World War is disproved by the detailed planning and preparation that in fact took place. An example of this is the work to safeguard museum artefacts and painting, which was in full swing by 1938. In June of that year, London Transport granted the government a licence for 'emergency storage of articles' at two disused tube stations (Dover Street and Brompton Road). In the event these locations were not used and instead the British Museum, the Tate

Gallery and the London Museum were allocated storage accommodation in disused passages at Piccadilly Circus station. At the same time the British Museum and Public Record Office were given joint custody of the Aldwych branch of the Piccadilly line, which was closed to trains from 1940 to 1946. Although many national treasures were relocated to Wales, Northamptonshire and Yorkshire, the great weight (100 tons) of the famous Elgin Marbles (or Parthenon Sculptures) meant that once they had been moved to the depths of Aldwych station, there they remained until April 1946.

After nearly seven years of safekeeping in the depths of Piccadilly Circus tube station priceless paintings are brought to the surface as passengers stare. The last paintings were returned to the Tate Gallery and London Museum on 5 February 1946.

The Adelphi Arches, two minutes' walk from the busy Strand, are one of the strangest and least visited sights of London. They are the oldest part of a quarter-mile of subterranean streets that never see the light of day.

Two underground streets

Location: Hungerford Lane and Lower Robert Street, both WC2N.

Still exists? Yes.

Accessible? Yes.

Hungerford Lane is a long-established thoroughfare, the site of which was built over when Charing Cross railway station was built in 1863. The road was then diverted to the western side of the station. If you stand in the station forecourt looking south and walk towards the far right-hand (western) side of the station, you will come upon a narrow passageway that is the northern entrance to Hungerford Lane. The other (southern) end of the lane runs into Villiers Street. Technically the lane is now a private road (distinguished by notices warning that you may be arrested if you do not move on when ordered) and is gated at times. All the same, it provides access to a nightclub and other premises.

Not far away is Lower Robert Street, the last fragment of London's 'underground village'. The 'dark arches' that Charles Dickens described in *David Copperfield* were in fact a handful of 'underground streets' that stood beneath the Adelphi, south of the Strand. Researcher Roger Morgan explains that when the Adam brothers developed the area in 1773 to create a block of twenty-four neo-classical terraced houses called the Adelphi Buildings, they levelled off the slope down to the Thames by constructing a huge sub-basement on a labyrinth of brick arches, with 'Lower' versions of the 'ground level' streets John Adam Street, Adam Street and Robert Street, together with Durham Street (which had no above-ground equivalent). When the central block of this development was redeveloped by the 'savagely ungraceful' New Adelphi office block in 1936, all these lower streets were rebuilt in rectangular concrete. However, a very short stretch of the original brick vaulted street still remains. It connects York Buildings to the new Lower Robert Street, giving a good impression of what the whole thing must have been like. In addition the Royal Society of Arts (under which Durham Street burrowed) has converted the north end into an auditorium, retaining the pavements, granite setts and the brick arched tunnel.

There is also a street called Lower Road that runs under Waterloo station, although this is at ground level and is covered by the station. Of course the same could be argued of Hungerford Lane.

This sombre and rather scruffy-looking covered roadway is all that remains of an ancient highway called Hungerford Lane, lost when Charing Cross station was built in the 1860s.

Further reading and useful websites can be found at www.shirebooks.co.uk/articles/additionalcontent

Index